Building Character

Showing Generosity

by Rebecca Pettiford

P9-DGE-459
DISCARD

Bullfrog Books

Ideas for Parents and Teachers

Bullfrog Books let children practice reading informational text at the earliest reading levels. Repetition, familiar words, and photo labels support early readers.

Before Reading

- Discuss the cover photo. What does it tell them?

- Look at the picture glossary together. Read and discuss the words.

Read the Book

- "Walk" through the book and look at the photos. Let the child ask questions. Point out the photo labels.

- Read the book to the child, or have him or her read independently.

After Reading

- Prompt the child to think more. Ask: How do you show generosity? How does it make you feel when you are generous?

Bullfrog Books are published by Jump!
5357 Penn Avenue South
Minneapolis, MN 55419
www.jumplibrary.com

Copyright © 2018 Jump! International copyright reserved in all countries. No part of this book may be reproduced in any form without written permission from the publisher.

Library of Congress Cataloging-in-Publication Data

Names: Pettiford, Rebecca, author.
Title: Showing generosity / by Rebecca Pettiford.
Description: Minneapolis, Minnesota: Jump!, Inc., 2018. | Series: Building character | Includes index.
Identifiers: LCCN 2017027972 (print)
LCCN 2017028561 (ebook)
ISBN 9781624966460 (ebook)
ISBN 9781620318843 (hardcover: alk. paper)
ISBN 9781620318850 (pbk.)
Subjects: LCSH: Generosity—Juvenile literature.
Classification: LCC BJ1533.G4 (ebook)
LCC BJ1533.G4 P48 2017 (print) | DDC 179/.9—dc23
LC record available at https://lccn.loc.gov/2017027972

Editor: Kirsten Chang
Book Designer: Michelle Sonnek
Photo Researchers: Michelle Sonnek & Kirsten Chang

Photo Credits: Gelpi/Shutterstock, cover; Edward Lara/Shutterstock, 1; Africa Studio/Shutterstock, 3, 11, 22 (jar); adriaticfoto/Shutterstock, 4; Blend Images/SuperStock, 5, 6–7, 16–17, 23tl, 23br; Sergiy Bykhunenko/Shutterstock, 6; Olha Tsiplyar/Shutterstock, 8–9, 23tr; akiyoko/Shutterstock, 10 (foreground), 23bl; Artazum/Shutterstock, 10 (background), 23bl; Steve Debenport/iStock, 12–13; pathdoc/Shutterstock, 14; NotarYES/Shutterstock, 15; Wavebreakmedia Ltd PH60/Alamy, 18–19; asiseeit/Getty, 20–21; Steve Cordory/Shutterstock, 22 (ribbon); Halfbottle/Shutterstock, 24.

Printed in the United States of America at Corporate Graphics in North Mankato, Minnesota.

Table of Contents

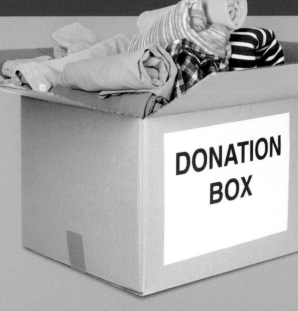

The Gift of Giving

We like to show generosity.

Being generous means giving because we want to.

We give things.

We give our time.

Bev gathers used books.

She gives them
to the library.

Others will be
able to read them.

library

Amy forgot her snack.
Ty shares his apple.

We have a new neighbor.

neighbor

We give her cookies.
"Welcome!"

11

Maya is generous
with her sister.

She reads her
a story.

She shares toys.

Oh no! Mr. Tom is sick.

He needs help.

14

Dan walks his dog.

We work in a soup kitchen.

We serve food to people who need it.

Al's mom had a hard day.

He helps her cook dinner.

It feels good to give!

Giving Jar

It feels good to give to others. This activity will help remind you to show generosity.

You will need:

- a clean glass jar
- stickers or ribbon

Directions:

1. Decorate your jar with stickers or ribbon.
2. Each time you get money, put a little into the jar.
3. When the jar is full, give the money to a charity. A charity is a group that helps people or animals. Examples are a soup kitchen or an animal shelter.

Picture Glossary

library
A building with books and other materials in it.

snack
A small amount of food eaten between meals.

neighbor
A person who lives next to or near another person.

soup kitchen
A place that gives food to people who need it.

Index

To Learn More

Learning more is as easy as 1, 2, 3.

1) Go to www.factsurfer.com

2) Enter "showinggenerosity" into the search box.

3) Click the "Surf" button to see a list of websites.

With factsurfer.com, finding more information is just a click away.